The Art of Sugarcraft

SUGAR FLOWERS

NICHOLAS LODGE

Foreword June Elwood
Series Editor Joyce Becker
Photography by Melvin Grey and Graham Tann

CHANCELLOR
PRESS

DL

Published in 1996 by Chancellor Press
an imprint of Reed Books Ltd
Michelin House, 81 Fulham Road
London SW3 6RB
and Auckland, Melbourne, Singapore and Toronto

By arrangement with Merehurst Limited
Ferry House, 51-57 Lacy Road, London, SW15 1PR
© Copyright 1986 Merehurst Limited

ISBN 1-85152-964-0

Designed by Carole Perks

Editorial Assistant Suzanne Ellis

Further assistance provided by Trudie Ballantyne, Susan Conder,
Rachel Lalley and Sara Townsend

Cover photograph by Graham Tann

Typeset by Filmset & Clive Dorman & Co.

Colour separation by Fotographics Ltd, U.K. – Hong Kong

Printed in Italy

CONTENTS

FOREWORD

As an avid collector of books on all aspects of cake artistry, I simply cannot wait for the publication of this book so that I may have my very own copy. I have on my shelves many books on the subject, published at various times and in different countries, but this book deals so comprehensively with the various techniques of making edible flowers and of using fresh flowers that I have no hesitation in saying that it is unique. It is not confined to techniques known and used in the United Kingdom, but includes some from other countries, for example the making of buttercream flowers, which though favoured in the United States is relatively unknown here. I therefore commend this book unreservedly to anyone who is seriously interested in the art of cake decorating.

Over the years I have known Nick Lodge I have seen him develop and refine his skills and techniques. I am delighted therefore that he has chosen to share his knowledge with a wider public. The reader has merely to leaf over the pages that follow to appreciate both the range of techniques covered, and the quality of their illustration and presentation. I have not the least doubt that this book will reach cake decorating enthusiasts in many lands, and will soon be regarded as a classic in its field. I wish its author every success in the future.

JUNE ELWOOD, M.C.F.A.(C.G.), M.Inst.B.B.

Nicholas Lodge is one of the brightest lights in the young generation of sugarcraft artists. Although still in his twenties, he already has an impressive collection of awards for his outstanding skills in the field of cake decoration and is one of the best selling authors of cake decorating books in the world today.

Nicholas studied cake decoration at the National Bakery School, London, where he was awarded the prize for the best decoration student. He then worked in a bakery to gain practical experience before joining one of Britain's leading commercial cake decorating firms as Principal Designer. Nicholas is now Creative Director of The House of Sugarcraft and is responsible for the cake decorating products that bear his name and are sold internationally.

He has taught sugarcraft to students at all levels as well as demonstrating sugarcraft in shops and department stores all over the UK. In addition, he has taught cake decorating in Singapore, Malaysia, Indonesia, Japan, and southern Africa.

In 1986 Nicholas wrote *Sugar Flowers* and co-authored *Chocolate* in THE ART OF SUGARCRAFT series. He has plans for more books in the future.

The House of Sugarcraft International School, of which Nicholas is the Principal, has affiliations with ten other schools worldwide, where Nicholas teaches for part of each year.

Nicholas is married and lives in Bournemouth.

SUGAR FLOWERS

This book is about making and using flowers in sugarcraft. It explains in detail how to make every kind of sugar flower — piped, moulded, cutter and wired — and how to use them in cake decoration. The use of fresh, dried and fabric flowers is also explained. Many new and diffe-rent techniques are covered, and every idea is illustrated with clear, step-by-step colour photographs.

The book also presents many different ideas for using sugar flowers, and new and different styles for cakes. As with all aspects of sugarart, many techniques described here are simply guidelines. There are few rules for cake decorating, and most skills come down to a matter of personal preference. Experiment to find the methods that work best for you, and the ideas and designs that you most enjoy creating.

Of course, to be a good sugar-craft artist you will need an all round general knowledge of decorating skills. Beautiful sugar flowers and sprays need to be displayed on expertly covered and decorated cakes. Experiment with the different covering mediums, remembering again that there are very few rules. Sugar flowers can look equally good on sugarpasted or royal iced cakes.

The style of flowers used on a cake will depend on the overall style and design of the cake. When designing a cake, the first things to consider are the occasion, the number of portions required and the shape. Although most people prefer round or square cakes, there are now many different-shaped tins on the market.

Hints and tips

Flower paste and modelling paste are affected by the warmth of your hands. A cake decorator with very warm hands would need to use a slightly firmer paste than someone with cold hands.

Always colour pastes with paste food colourings, not liquid ones, which will change the consistency of the modelling pastes. Add the colour using the end of a cocktail stick, and always use a new cocktail stick whenever more colour is added.

After colouring flower paste or sugarpaste, put it in a plastic bag and return it to the refrigerator for a few minutes. Kneading in the colour will make the paste warm and stringy, and it will be difficult to use without chilling.

Many colours, particularly yellows and reds, will deepen on standing, so colour the paste a shade lighter than the desired finished colour.

An alternative method of colouring flowers is to make them all white, cream or a pale shade and then petal dust to the desired shade when dry.

Petal dust is a powdered food colouring based on cornflour (cornstarch), which can be mixed in with the petal dust to obtain a lighter shade.

When using petal dust or lustre colour on flowers, be sure that the cake is boxed or removed from the room, or the fine dust may float through the air and discolour the cake covering.

Flower paste should be rolled as thinly as possible so that the petals will be translucent and natural looking. Paste can be rolled out on a thin film of white fat (shortening) or on a light dusting of cornflour (cornstarch). Experiment to find which one works best for you.

When doing double frilling, as in an orchid throat or carnations, the paste should be slightly thicker than usual or it will not frill successfully.

If using cornflour (cornstarch) to dust the work surface, place it in a square of butter muslin tied in a bag, or use a pepper pot for a miniature flour dredger.

Colour is perhaps the most important factor in the look of a celebration cake. To some extent this is dependent on fashion, particularly with wedding cakes. Because many brides now wear ivory, cream or pastel-coloured dresses instead of white, it is becoming more popular to cover the cake in a shade to match the wedding dress, instead of with pure white icing.

If using dark or vibrant colours on the cake, make only the smallest flowers of the spray in the darkest shade. Larger flowers must be pale or they will look heavy. Coloured ribbon bands or bows, or ribbon loops in the sprays, can add additional bright colour.

Again, there are very few rules about colour. Blue is often very cold, but can be made warmer when used with peaches or pinks. Lemons and greens look very fresh and spring-like, and work very well on cakes. Use your eye and experiment to see which colours you prefer.

All flowers can be used either wired or unwired, depending on the style of the spray. In a South African-style spray every compo-nent must be wired, but in an Australian-style spray the larger flowers would be unwired and inserted into the base on the cake. Practise making the various sprays shown in this book to discover which ones work best for your style of decorating.

Hints and tips

Roll out only enough paste to cut two or three petals at a time. Flower paste dries out quickly, and if too many petals are cut at once it will be difficult to frill, shape or mould them.

Try to obtain examples of the flowers you are making from a garden or florist, particularly when making a new variety.

It is not necessary to pur-chase every available flower cutter. Metal cutters can be bent to different shapes with fine pliers.

Cutter flowers can be made by using cardboard tem-plates of the petals. Place the template on the rolled-out paste and cut round it with a modelling knife. This is a time-consuming method but useful if only a few flowers are being made.

When cutting out petals, the edges may look ragged. To avoid this, place the cutter on top of the rolled-out paste and apply enough pressure to cut through the paste. Turn the cutter upsidedown and gently run your finger along the edge of the cutter. Push the paste through and lift the cutter away.

Piped flowers and foliage, whether royal icing or buttercream, must be made from stiff icing or they will collapse. Add more icing (confectioner's) sugar to make the icing firm.

Never insert wires directly into the cake. Either place in a posy pick or insert them into a piece of sugarpaste on the cake surface.

When using fresh flowers in sprays or for making crystal-lized flowers, take care to use flowers which are safe to eat. Never use flowers which have been grown from bulbs. Consult a florist or a reliable reference book about the suitability of a

flower or plant, and if in any doubt do not use it on the cake.

Buy inexpensive fabric flowers to practise making up and wiring sprays. Fabric flowers are easier to work with than sugar flowers, and time is saved by not having to mould flowers.

When making a wedding cake, ask for details of the bridal bouquet and make the flowers for the cake to match.

SPECIAL EQUIPMENT
FOR SUGAR FLOWERS

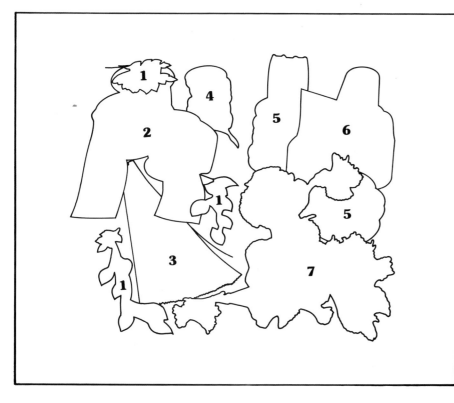

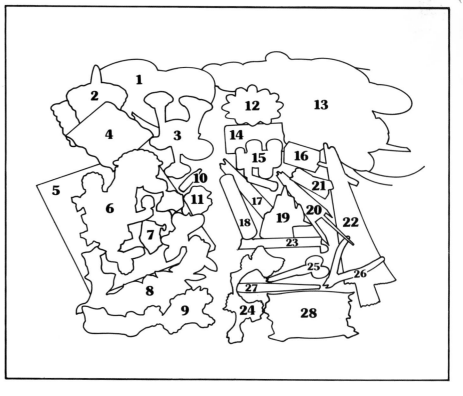

The equipment shown here is available from special suppliers and is used in floristry as well as for cake decorating.

1	Wired fabric leaves
2	Lantern ribbon for frills
3	Fabric-covered floristry wire
4	Floristry tape
5	Floristry ribbon
6	Tulle
7	Artificial stamens in various sizes and colours

This is a selection of tools and equipment used for making sugar flowers. Most are ordinary kitchen or household items, while the more unusual tools are available from cake decorating shops and specialist suppliers.

1	Cake boards
2	Basket for arrangements
3	Vases for arrangements
4	Form for drying flowers and leaves
5	Non-stick board
6	Cutters
7	Plunger cutters
8	Leaf veiners
9	Leaf cutters
10	Posy pick
11	Glass-headed pins
12	Posy frill
13	Ribbons
14	Artist's palette for drying or mixing colours
15	Paste colours and petal dust
16	Tape shredder
17	Paintbrushes
18	Rolling pin
19	Piping tubes and bags
20	Wooden skewers and sticks/ metal skewer
21	Cocktail sticks
22	Floristry wire
23	Modelling knife
24	Stamens
25	Scissors
26	Wire cutters
27	Tweezers
28	Modelling tools

FLOWER PASTE

All of the moulded flowers in this book have been made using this recipe for flower paste. However, there are many variations on this recipe, so experiment to find one which suits you. Remember that flower paste is affected by climate, and if you live in a very humid place, then you may need to add more cornflour (cornstarch) and reduce the amount of icing sugar.

425g (14oz/3½cups) icing (confectioner's) sugar, sifted
60g (2oz/¼cup) cornflour (cornstarch)
15ml (3 teaspoons) gum tragacanth
or
10ml (2 teaspoons) gum tragacanth and 10ml (2 teaspoons) carboxy methyl cellulose
25ml (5 teaspoons) cold water
10ml (2 teaspoons) powdered gelatine
15ml (3 teaspoons) white fat (shortening)
10ml (2 teaspoons) liquid glucose
white of one large egg, string removed

Sift together the sugar and cornflour in the bowl of a heavy-duty mixer. Sprinkle over the gum tragacanth, or the gum tragacanth and carboxy methyl cellulose.

Place the mixer bowl over a large pan of boiling water. Cover the top with a dry cloth, and then with a plate or cake board.

Put the water in a small glass bowl and sprinkle the powdered gelatine over it. Leave to sponge.

Half fill a small saucepan with water and place over low heat. Bring to just below the boiling point. Place the bowl of sponged gelatine, the container of liquid glucose and the beater from the mixer in the water. Heat until the gelatine is clear. Remove the bowl of gelatine from the pan and stir in the liquid glucose and the white fat. Stir until the fat is melted.

When the icing sugar feels warm, take the bowl off the pan of boiling water, dry the bottom, and place on the mixer. Remove the beater from the other pan, dry, and assemble the mixer. Add the gelatine solution and the egg white to the sugar. Cover the bowl with a cloth, and turn the mixer to the slowest speed. Mix until all the ingredients are combined and the paste is a dull beige colour.

Turn the mixer to maximum and beat until the paste is white and stringy. This will take 5-10 minutes. Remove the paste from the bowl and place in a clean plastic bag. Place the bag in an airtight container and refrigerate for at least 24 hours before using. If planning to store the paste for a few weeks, put it in four or five small bags and open one at a time.

To use the paste, cut off a small piece, add a smear of white fat and dip into some egg white before working. The warmth of your hands will bring the paste to a workable, elastic consistency. Remember that the paste dries out very quickly, so keep it covered at all times and never cut off more than a very small piece. Certain colours, particularly reds and violets, may change the consistency, so it may be necessary to add more white fat and egg white.

Quick flower paste
This paste is easier to make, but the flowers will not be as delicate.

225g (8oz) commercial sugarpaste
5ml (1 teaspoon) gum tragacanth
white fat (shortening)

Knead the sugarpaste and gum tragacanth together, adding a small amount of white fat to get an elastic consistency. Store and use as for the previous recipe.

ICING FOR FLOWERS

Royal Icing
Fresh egg method
1 large egg white, which has been cracked and left in the refrigerator to liquify for about 2 hours
300g (10oz/2½cups) sifted icing (confectioner's) sugar
pinch tartaric acid (cream of tartar)

Put the egg white in a large bowl. Gradually stir in half the sugar until the mixture is the consistency of unwhipped cream. Add the rest of the sugar, a spoonful at a time, stirring after each addition. Stir, do not beat until the icing stands in firm peaks when the spoon is withdrawn.

Albumen powder method
Albumen powder is available in pure or substitute forms. Pure 100% dried albumen is used for fine lace work, run-outs, etc. It is stronger than substitute albumen, which is only suitable for basic work.

15ml (1 tablespoon) albumen powder
75ml (3floz) cold water
480g (1lb/4cups) sifted icing (confectioner's) sugar

Dissolve the albumen powder in the cold water and leave to stand for about 30 minutes, stirring every few minutes. Put the sugar in the bowl of an electric mixer, add the dissolved albumen powder, and mix using the beater for about 12-15 minutes.

If using royal icing to coat a cake, it must rest for at least 6 hours to allow the air bubbles to come to the surface and break. Royal icing for piping can be used straight after mixing.

Buttercream for piped flowers

300g (10oz/1¼cups) white vegetable fat (shortening)
480g (1lb/4cups) icing (confectioner's) sugar
45ml (3 tablespoons) cold water
flavouring and colouring

Thoroughly blend together the fat and sugar. Add the cold water and flavouring and mix for about 5 minutes. Colour as desired.

Buttercream

This recipe is less good for piping and flowers than the previous one, but it has an excellent flavour and smooth texture and is good for coating gateaux and other cakes, or for a filling.

100g (4oz/½cup) butter
225g (8oz/2cups) sifted icing (confectioner's) sugar
15-30mls (3-6 teaspoons) milk or fruit juice
few drops vanilla or other flavouring

Beat the butter until very soft. Beat in the icing sugar a little at a time. Add enough liquid to get the desired consistency and the flavouring, and beat until all the ingredients are well blended and very creamy.

PIPED FLOWER CAKE

This design can be adapted for
many different occasions, and is
suitable for any sized cake. It can
be used on sugarpaste, as shown,
or on a royal-iced cake.

PIPED FLOWERS

Piped flowers can be made in many different varieties, shapes and sizes. Flowers can either be piped onto flower nails, or onto squares of wax paper stuck onto the work surface. Cut several 2.5cm (1in) squares of wax paper before beginning. Flowers are piped with a petal nozzle, and these are available in right-handed and left-handed versions. Piping perfect flowers takes a lot of practise to know how to maintain the correct pressure and learn when to release pressure. The icing must be fairly firm, so that the flowers hold their shape.

Rotate the wax paper and pipe the second petal.

Rotate the wax paper and pipe the third petal. You should have covered two-thirds of the circumference of the flower. If not, the petals are either too fat or too thin.

Rotate the wax paper and pipe the fourth petal.

Rotate the wax paper and pipe the fifth petal, release pressure and carefully lift the bag away. Pipe a small dot in the centre using a contrasting colour and a small tube. This is a basic piped blossom.

Place a square of wax paper on the work surface. Place the petal nozzle in the end of a bag and fill with stiff royal icing. The thicker end of the nozzle should always be towards the centre of the flower. Start off piping, using your wrist to give the flow to the petals, and keeping an even pressure. Pipe a tight horseshoe shape.

MORE PIPED FLOWERS

Carnation: Pipe the round basic shape. Using a fine, moist paintbrush, feather the ends of the petals while the icing is still wet. Pipe calyx when slightly dry.

Bess rose: This is similar to the basic piped blossom. Half-way through piping each petal, quickly move your wrist back and forth to make the heart-shaped petals. This rose has been piped using a technique called colour flow, which means that the piping bag has been filled with two or three colours of icing, in this case pink and white.

Violet: This is just a variation on the basic piped blossom. Study the shape and pipe with violet-coloured icing.

Daisy: Use the same technique as for the basic blossom, but go up and down instead of making a horseshoe, and make more petals.

Rose: Hold the piping bag so that the nozzle is standing up. Start with a central cone, then three vertical petals. Pipe the outer petals as for the basic blossom.

Pansy: Using the colour flow technique, pipe the first two petals as for the basic blossom. Pipe over them again, then pipe one petal opposite the first two.

Sweet pea: Holding the bag as for the blossom, pipe a horseshoe shape, then a smaller one inside. With the tube down on the paper, pipe a small stem. Pipe the calyx with a No2 tube.

BUTTERCREAM CATTLEYA ORCHID

The cattleya orchid here and all of the buttercream flowers on the following pages have been piped with a No59 tube, but another petal tube could also be used. Use the buttercream recipe made with white fat (shortening) on page 11 for best results. The orchid can either be made as shown, with the base petals a different colour from the tongue, or by the colour flow method, using two colours in the same bag.

Take a piece of wax paper and mark a centre dot with a pencil. To make the first petal, pipe a shell about 4cm (1½in) long from the dot to the outside edge with a petal tube. Pipe a flat line of buttercream up either side of the shell.

Pipe two more petals in the arrangement shown, exactly as for the first petal.

Pipe the upper two halves of the frilled petals. Keep the thick end of the nozzle towards the centre and move your hand backwards and forwards to make a frilled edge.

Make the bottom halves in the same way. Pull a small paintbrush down the centre of each petal to make the vein. Refrigerate for 10 minutes.

For the tongue, pipe three horseshoe shapes upside-down as you look on towards the top petal. Pipe a frilly edge around the outside of each one.

Pipe the column in the centre of the tongue using a small bag and a No2 tube. Mark two holes in the end of the column with a cocktail stick. When the orchid is dry, paint on any additional colouring with oil-based food colouring or petal dust.

MORE BUTTERCREAM FLOWERS

Blossom: Pipe five horseshoe-shaped buttercream petals, exactly as for the step-by-step royal icing blossom on page 13.

Sweet pea: Pipe the outer petals in two halves. Pipe the central horseshoe-shape, then a small shell-shaped bud. Dry, then pipe on a green calyx with a No2 tube.

Briar rose: Pipe as for the blossom, but make the petals heart-shaped by flicking your wrist back and forth at the top of each petal. Pipe some yellow stamens in the centre, and dust with green petal dust.

Carnation: Pipe a ring of buttercream, keeping the narrow end towards the outside, and moving the tube back and forth to give a frilled edge. Pipe single frilled petals to fill the centre, working in a clockwise direction. Refrigerate until firm. Carefully remove the flower from the wax paper, turn over and make a calyx by piping a pulled-up star with a No7 tube.

Arum lily: Pipe a petal-shape in white butter-cream. Pipe a yellow pistil with a No3 tube. Using the white icing, join a strip to the petal shape, fold either side over to cover the base of the pistil. Dry, then pipe on a green calyx.

Daffodil: Pipe the six petals, then pull a small paintbrush down the centre of each one and pinch the ends to make a slight point. Refrigerate for a few minutes. Pipe a circle for the trumpet by holding the tube upright with the thicker end at the base and pulling as you pipe to make the frilled edge. Pipe some green stamens in the centre of the trumpet.

Buttercream foliage piped with a leaf tube.

PHILIPPINE WIRED FLOWERS

These small Philippine-style flowers make lovely additions to both sugar and fabric flower sprays. They are very quick to make, and they are most useful for softening sprays, and for enlarging or adding height to top ornaments.

Bend 28- or 30-gauge covered wire into soft curves. This must be done before piping the flowers, as the flowers might break or fall off if the wire is bent afterwards. Place the bent wire on wax paper.

The flowers and foliage are piped with a No1 tube. Copy the ones shown here, or pipe similar tiny flowers from fresh flowers. Leave to dry thoroughly.

Peel carefully off the wax paper, starting from the end of the wire. If double-sided flowers are required, turn over and pipe on the other side.

SUGARPASTE ROSES

Sugarpaste roses are easy-to-make decorations for cakes and confectionery. If making coloured roses, knead the colour through the sugarpaste, then leave the paste to rest for about 15 minutes. Colouring the paste makes it very soft and stringy, but resting will return it to the original consistency.

Make three more petals. Position one on the cone opposite the point where the first petal overlaps. Attach the left-hand side to the first petal and leave the right-hand side open. Repeat for the second petal, tucking each under and over.

Attach the third petal by tucking it inside the second petal and over top of the first. Waist in the base to establish the shape. For a rose bud, cut off the cone now using scissors or a sharp knife.

If making a full rose, make another row of three petals, attaching them as before.

To make larger roses, continue adding petals, following the same formation. A fully-blown rose will have 19 petals. When the rose is the desired size, cut it off the cone using a sharp knife or scissors. Leave to dry thoroughly before placing them on a cake.

Take a pea-sized piece of paste and roll it in the palm of your hand. Flatten it between a folded piece of polythene by using your thumb and pulling away from yourself. Thin out about two-thirds of the paste, retaining the thicker base. This is the first petal.

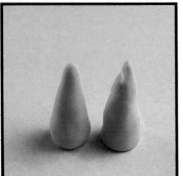

Make a cone of sugarpaste and wrap the first petal completely around it. The cone should not be visible.

HEART WEDDING CAKE

This two-tiered heart-shaped wedding cake features a sugar flower spray made to match the bridal bouquet.

FRESH FLOWERS

A basic knowledge of floristry is useful to the sugarcraft artist. Sugar flower sprays are made using the same basic principles of floristry, and most sugarcraft artists who make sugar flowers also enjoy arranging fresh flowers.

A pink and white brides-maid's posy featuring roses, carnations and freesias.

A bridal bouquet featuring moth orchids and yellow carnations. The filler flowers are individual freesias and gypsophila, offset by spring foliage and matching ribbons.

A traditional cascading bridal bouquet.

Fresh flowers in a silver vase, which could be used on top of a tiered wedding cake or as a table decoration.

Always take care to use suitable varieties when choosing flowers to decorate food. There are some plants and flowers which are poisonous, so take care to avoid them. Never place flowers grown from bulbs directly on food. A good florist should be able to advise which varieties are safe.

Most flowers will not last very long out of water, so try to use those that will keep if they are to be placed directly on the cake. If fresh flowers are to be placed in a vase on top of a cake, fill the vase with florist's foam which has been soaked for several hours in cool water. Place soaked florist's foam in the bottom of a posy pick if a spray is to be inserted into a cake.

Try to avoid flowers which have a lot of pollen, as the cake will soon be covered with the yellow pollen dust. Again, the florist should be able to advise on the varieties which quickly shed pollen.

A cake decorator may be asked to match the bridal bouquet or bridesmaid's posy with a sugar flower arrangement. Discuss with the florist which flowers will be used. For a co-ordinated look, try to match the ribbons on the cake and sprays with the ribbons used in the bouquets. This is particularly important if the florist is making a spray to go in a vase on top of the wedding cake.

With practice, a skilled sugar artist will be able to make bouquets from both fresh flowers and sugar flowers.

WEDDING CAKE
WITH FRESH
FLOWERS

CRYSTALLIZED FLOWERS

Crystallized flowers are easy to make and are attractive decorations for cakes, serving trays and other food.

As with all fresh flower work, choose the varieties carefully. Roses, violets and fruit-tree blossom are the most suitable types for crystallizing. Never use any flower which has been grown from a bulb. The flowers should have just opened and must be completely dry. For soft-stemmed flowers such as violets, cut off the stem and hold with fine-pointed tweezers.

Store crystallized flowers between layers of tissue paper in an airtight tin. If kept in a cool place, they will keep for several months.

Crystallized flowers look best when arranged in a little bunch, as shown here. Pipe on the stem with a No1 or No2 tube and finish the spray with a bow.

Designs using commercially prepared crystallized rose petals, violets and mimosa. Pipe the stems and leaves with royal icing.

Lightly whisk some egg white, and use a medium-sized paintbrush to completely cover the flower petals and calyx. Sprinkle the flower with caster sugar. The sugar can be coloured to match the flower by mixing in a little petal dust.

Shake off any excess sugar and dry the flowers completely. Smaller varieties can be left to dry on kitchen paper. For larger flowers and for roses, wrap a piece of wire around the stem and dry hanging upside-down to avoid squashing the petals.

FORTIETH ANNIVERSARY OR BIRTHDAY CAKE

This square cake features a posy
made from dried miniature red
roses.

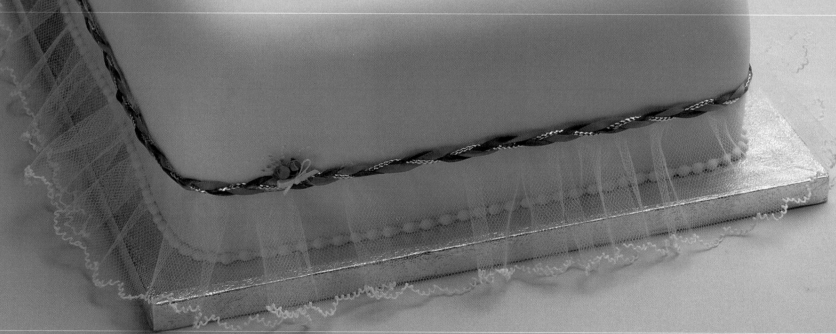

DRIED FLOWERS

Although not very widely used by cake decorators, dried flowers can be used as an alternative to sugar flowers or fresh flowers in an arrangement or spray.

In recent years, dried flowers have become very popular for winter floral arrangements, and department stores and florists now stock a vast assortment of dried flowers, seeds and grasses. It is also possible to dry flowers at home, although home-dried ones lose colour faster than those dried commercially.

For cake decorations, choose the smaller dried flowers, such as statice, rose buds and the tiny roses shown in the posy.

Because the stems are dehydrated they are very brittle and cannot be twisted into sprays. Remove the stems and put each flower on the end of a 28- or 30-gauge wire to make arranging the sprays easier. Dried sea lavender, which looks like gypsophila, makes a good base for small dried sprays, and it can be used in small pieces without wired stems.

The dried flower arrangements shown on these pages are made in the same way as the sugar flower sprays. If a dried flower spray is to go on top of a cake, always place it in a posy pick to prevent the flowers from coming in contact with the cake.

Dried flowers arranged in a silver vase which could be placed on top of a cake or used as a table centre.

A basket arrangement of dried flowers.

Dried flower posies. To use on top of a cake, place in a posy pick inserted in the cake surface.

FABRIC FLOWERS

Fabric flowers have many different uses in cake decorating. Attractive and dramatic effects can be created by a fabric flower spray on a celebration cake.

Ribbon is available from specialist suppliers for making your own individually designed fabric flowers.

Department stores, florists and cake decorating suppliers now stock an enormous range of fabric flowers, from tiny miniature buds and blossom to fully opened orchids and lilies. The most realistic, and most expensive, ones are made from silk, but attractive synthetic fabric flowers are also available.

One excellent use for fabric flowers is to practise wiring sprays. Fabric flowers are less fragile than sugar flowers, and using them for practice saves the time of moulding flowers. For all fabric flower work, cut the heads off first, as they tend to be on thick wires, and tape them onto 24- or 26-gauge wire.

When choosing fabric flowers for a spray, take along the ribbons and try to match the colours. If planning a spray with pale or delicate shades, a better effect can be achieved by buying white flowers and petal dusting the edges, rather than using coloured flowers, which can look harsh.

Silk flowers can be wired into the traditional sprays or placed in vases. Try experimenting by making sprays with a combination of fabric and sugar flowers. For example, replace the gypsophila, which is a time-consuming sugar flower to make, with silk gypsophila, or use silk foliage to set off sugar roses.

A silver vase filled with cascading silk flowers.

A bridal bouquet featuring
silk orchids.

Fabric flowers arranged in
a wicker basket.

A traditional arrangement
of fabric flowers in a vase.

PINK BIRTHDAY CAKE

This round cake is suitable
for a birthday or other occasion.

MOULDED FLOWERS

There are two distinctly different ways of making modelled flower paste flowers — hand-moulding and using cutters. Most sugar flower sprays include both types successfully, although if entering a competition check the schedule carefully to see if this is allowed.

Pulled flowers: Hand-moulded flowers are usually known as pulled flowers, and they are the easiest moulded flowers to make. No special equipment is required, only a sharp modelling knife and wooden modelling sticks. Pulled flowers can be made in miniature or life-sized. The smaller the piece of paste used, the smaller the finished flower will be.

Cutter flowers: Cutter flowers are made by rolling out the flower paste and cutting it out with a cutter before shaping or frilling. Metal and plastic flower cutters are available in many different shapes and sizes. However, it is not necessary to acquire every cutter, as a skilled decorator can learn to bend cutters using pliers and to shape the paste for a particular petal once it has been cut from another petal shape.

Always try to make cutter flowers by working from a real flower. Pull off a petal and find a cutter which is close to its shape. If no cutter is available, either bend another cutter or make one from a sheet of thin metal.

As cutters are expensive, store them carefully packed in a box to prevent them from getting bent out of shape. Keep them clean, and if you wash them, dry immediately. Plastic cutters are less fragile, but take care not to damage them with sharp modelling tools.

A bridal bouquet made with cutter and pulled flowers.

Doris pinks made by the same technique for carnations.

WIRED ROSE

The rose is the most commonly used flower in cake decorating, and there are many different ways of making roses, depending on how they are to be used. The wired roses shown here are mainly used in sprays. To make realistic roses, start with paste in a fairly dark colour, then add a bit of white paste after each layer so that the rose is shaded from a dark centre cone to pale outer petals.

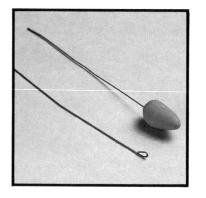

Make a hook in the end of a piece of 26-gauge wire, dip into egg white, and mould a cone of flower paste around it.

Roll out some paste and cut two petals using a rose petal cutter. Slightly soften with a cocktail stick. Wrap one petal around the cone and stick with a little egg white. Wrap the second petal around so that it sits in the flap of the first petal.

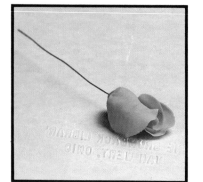

Add some white to the coloured paste and roll out enough to cut three petals. Soften to frill slightly and cup by using a cranked ball tool. Wrap the petals around the first layer, tucking the first petal in the overlap of the previous row. The second petal goes in the flap of the first and the third petal goes in the flap of the second and on top of the first.

Cut five petals of the palest paste for the outer row. Soften, cup slightly, and assemble as for the previous layers. Leave to dry for about 30 minutes.

Make the calyx by making a small hat shape from pale green paste. Roll out the edges, but keep the centre node. Cut as shown, thread onto the wire and mould slightly onto the base of the rose.

When dry, petal dust the rose to bring out highlights. Dust the inside part of the calyx with white petal dust for a two-tone effect.

MORE ROSES

All of these rose corsages have a wired rose as the focal point. The simplest one features an orange-red rose with ribbon loops and a spray of gypsophila. The large pink rose is wired with an assortment of ivy, pulled blossom, gypsophila and ribbons. A spray for a small cake features a full yellow rose and a half rose, combined with pulled blossom and foliage. Add ribbon loops to fill out the rounded shape.

ANEMONE

Anemones come in a range of colours: red, pink, cerise, violet, blue and cream. They are made with cutters and assembled by the shallow dish method. Use patty tins or pans or polystyrene trays used to pack apples for shipping.

When flowers and foliage are completely dry, assemble with the leaves arranged around the base of the flowers. If making a wired spray, attach to the main stem with a small amount of floristry tape.

Lightly grease the shallow dish with white vegetable fat. Roll out and cut a pale green calyx. If making wired anemones, make a slight cone in the base for the wire and insert wire.

Roll out the coloured paste very thinly and cut six petals using a rose petal cutter. Taking each petal in turn, soften the edges with a cocktail stick, texture with a violet leaf veiner, then place on a dry sponge and cup slightly with a ball tool. Place upturned in an ice cube tray or something similar. When you have finished all six petals, start assembling with the first petal made.

Assemble on top of the calyx in the prepared shallow dish. Roll out another piece of paste and cut four or five more petals. Treat as in Step 2, then assemble on top of the first layer, making a total of 10 or 11 petals. Leave to dry.

If making an anemone with white detail, mix white petal dust with clear spirit and paint it in with a fine paintbrush. To make the stamen, place a small ball of paste on your forefinger and texture by pulling a small piece of tulle over it. Cover with black stamens and pieces of stamen cotton. Position in the centre of the petals. If not adding white detail, place stamen in the centre as soon as the flower is assembled.

Anemone foliage is made with a crysanthemum leaf cutter. Cut using only the top half of the cutter, make as for variegated ivy, insert the wire, and leave to dry in a natural curve by supporting on foam. Varnish for effect.

SHALLOW DISH FLOWERS

Christmas rose: Cut a green calyx and place in the shallow dish. Cut five white petals using a rose or Christmas rose cutter. Soften, cup and assemble as for the poppy. Position yellow stamens on a base in the centre. When dry, lightly dust green around the base and stamens.

Fully blown rose: Cut a green calyx and place in the shallow dish. Choose three sizes of rose cutter, and cut five petals with each one. Soften and cup all the petals. Arrange in three layers in the dish, starting with the largest petals and finishing with the smallest. Place yellow stamens in the centre. Petal dust the dry flower.

Scabious: Lightly grease a shallow dish. Roll out blue paste very thinly and cut two circles with a round cutter. Frill the edges with a cocktail stick and place one on top of the other in the dish. Roll some strips of white paste, frill, and arrange in a ring in the centre. Make some tiny cones and attach to the centre with egg white. Place a few stamens in the centre of the flower. When dry, dust the centre with green petal dust.

Briar rose: Cut a green calyx and place in the shallow dish. Roll out white paste and cut five petals with a heart cutter. Assemble as for the poppy. Place a ring of yellow flower paste in the centre and fill with yellow stamens. Texture a piece of paste with some tulle and place in the very centre.

Poppy: Cut a green calyx using a small rose calyx cutter and place in the shallow dish. Cut five red petals with a rose petal cutter. Soften the edge and cup onto foam. Place the petals, one at a time, onto the calyx and stick with a little egg white. The fifth petal should be placed overlapping the

fourth and tucked under the first. Make the centre from a ball of yellow paste. Attach two rings of black stamens. Position a green paste stigma in the centre.

Water lily: These flowers can be pink, white, lilac or yellow. Make two or three shades of paste before beginning, so that the flower is darker in the centre. Use a water lily petal cutter to cut about ten petals from the palest paste. Soften, cup and place in the dish. Cut more petals from slightly darker paste and assemble in another layer on top. Continue until the desired effect is achieved. Attach stamens in the centre. Cut the leaf with a water lily leaf cutter. Soften, vein, and then soften the edges with a cocktail stick.

PHALAENOPSIS ORCHID

The Phalaenopsis, or moth, orchid comes in white, pinks, lilac and green. If making coloured flowers, colour the flower paste in a pale shade of the chosen colour, as it is difficult to dust the assembled flower because of the shape. Roll out a small cone of paste very thinly, retaining the centre cone, cut the node in half, and slightly cup each half.

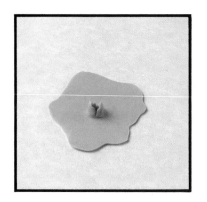

Using a lip cutter, cut out the centre lip, positioning the node in the centre of the cutter.

Slightly frill the two wing petals, then split the pointed petal in half. Roll the top petal into a thin tube and stick with egg white. Place in a small artist's palette to dry.

Make a former from thin metal, such as an empty drink can. The former should be slightly larger than the sepal cutter used. Roll out another piece of paste and cut the three sepals with the sepal cutter. Slightly soften the edges with a cocktail stick. Place each sepal in turn on a violet leaf veiner and gently rub over the paste with the index finger. Place the sepals on the metal former to dry.

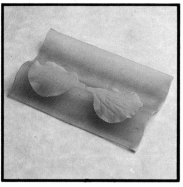

Roll out another piece of paste and cut one of the wing petals. Turn the cutter over and cut another, so that you have a pair of petals. Soften, vein and place on a curved surface to dry.

All pieces must be dry before assembling the orchid. Colour royal icing or softened flower paste to match the shade of the paste. Assemble the two wing petals, then attach the lip petal to the centre with royal icing. Mould a column with a cupped end and attach to the centre of the orchid. Petal dust and paint additional colour and shading to create a realistic flower.

PAPHIOPEDILUM

Also called slipper orchid or lady's slipper, this is an unusual sugar flower. Roll out some white paste and cut one petal using a large rose petal cutter. Soften with a cocktail stick, then place onto a large violet leaf veiner. Transfer to a sponge and mark down the centre with a veining tool. Place on a cupped surface.

Bend a medium-sized rose petal cutter and cut out the two wing petals. Treat as for the first petal. Put each petal on a cupped surface and place a ball of cotton wool to support each large end.

Cut out the base petal using a medium-large rose petal cutter. Soften, vein, and dry upturned on a curved surface.

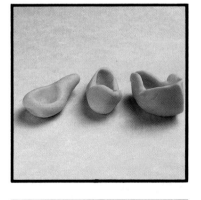

Assemble the four petals as shown and attach with a little royal icing. Leave to dry, then petal dust with lemon and pink and paint on the dots using dark plum colouring.

Mould the lip as shown, cup the petal and leave to dry. Petal dust, then attach to the centre of the flower using flower paste softened with egg white. Support with foam.

Make the column by moulding a small cone of paste and squashing the end. Attach to the centre and add two small frilled pieces to the end. Petal dust when dry.

MORE ORCHIDS

All of these orchids are made in a similar way to the Phalaenopsis and Paphiopedilum orchids, shown step-by-step on the previous pages.

Pansy orchid: Similar to the vanda orchid, these flowers are more like a pansy than an orchid, which is how they have acquired the name. Make with cutters and assemble as shown for the other orchids.

Cymbidium: This is a popular orchid for bridal bouquets and wedding cakes. It can be made with fixed petals or by wiring. Wired petals are easier to arrange in a finished spray. Practice is needed in shaping the tongue and lip to get a realistic look. Cymbidiums come in a wide range of colours, including very unusual green and dark gold shades.

Vanda orchid: These are easy to make using the wing petal cutter from the Phalaenopsis orchid. Assemble them in the same way. Although not common in cake decoration, they come in lovely shades of pink, peach and mauve, often with beautiful markings, and look attractive in sprays.

Cattleya: The easiest orchid to make, these are based on the same principles as the Garrett frill. Like the cymbidium, they can either be wired or unwired, with the wired orchids being easier to arrange in sprays. Cattleyas come in shades of pink, lilac and white, and are traditional in American bridal sprays.

Dendrobium: The Dendrobium is commonly known as the Singapore orchid, and it is becoming very popular in sugarcraft. Although made with the same cutters as the cattleya, the petals are not frilled. It comes in many colours, although the ivory and pink is the most common one.

ALSTROEMERIA

These large, trumpet-shaped flowers work well in sprays which are assembled directly onto the cake, as in Australian-style sprays which have a small sausage of sugarpaste as a base. They can also be wired. Alstroemeria come in many shades of yellow, red, cream and pink.

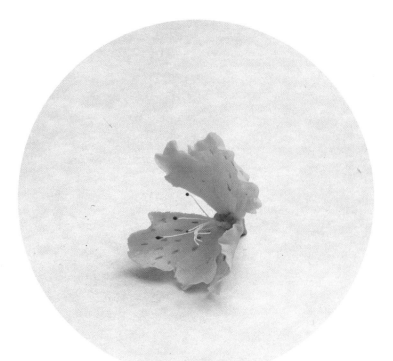

First make a former from foil, or use a small funnel. Cut a circle of foil and make it into a cone.

To assemble, place one petal in between two of the outer petals. Place the other two petals together at the top of the flower.

To make the petals, bend an azalea cutter with pliers to get the correct shape. Roll out some paste and cut three petals. Take each petal and vein with three lines. Frill the square end, pull a tiny lip in the centre, and curl over the edges slightly. Cup with a ball tool.

Assemble the three petals in the foil cone. Stick with a little egg white where they overlap.

For the three inside petals, bend a freesia cutter, cut, and treat as for the outer petals.

Wire together three white stamens and then four brown stamens. Tape both sets together, and position in the centre of the petals. Petal dust the dry flower and paint in the markings on the petals. Attach a small cone of green paste to the base for the calyx. The cone could contain a piece of wire if the flowers are to be wired into a spray.

MORE TRUMPET-SHAPED FLOWERS

Bridal gladiolus: Roll out some pale pink or peach paste and cut four petals with an azalea cutter. Soften, insert wires, and place over a small rolling pin to dry. Wire the petals together. Cut two more petals, soften, and attach to the flower. Position the stamens. When dry, petal dust the flower and cover the wires with floristry tape.

Rubrum lily: Roll out the paste using a paintbrush as for variegated ivy, retaining a thicker part. Cut out six petals, keeping a thicker piece at the base. Insert a wire into the thicker portion, and place the petals on a sponge, cupping slightly until dry. Twist the wires together and cover with floristry tape. Petal dust and paint on the dots with food colouring. For stamens, mould some paste onto the wire and dust.

Tiger lily: Cut out three petals from orange paste using an azalea cutter. Soften the edges, then arrange in a foil cone, leaving gaps between the petals. Cut three more petals and position on top of the first row. Stick tiny pieces of orange paste on the ends of some stamens and place these in the flower. Petal dust when dry and paint in spots with brown food colouring.

Scarborough lily: Roll out some pink or red paste and cut three petals. Mark lines all over the petals with a veiner and soften the top with a cocktail stick. Assemble in a foil cone. Make three more petals and position these over the first layer. Position six stamens. Petal dust when dry.

Azalea: Cut out a petal using an azalea cutter and slightly frill it. Place on a sponge and mark the centre vein using a veiner or cocktail stick. Shape the petal by placing it on the table leaning against a wooden stick. Make four more petals. Assemble the five petals in a fan shape on the table and stick together with a little egg white. Drop into the foil cone and then stick

the fifth petal on top of the first. Position six half stamens and one three-quarter length stamen. When the flower is dry, petal dust and paint spots on the throat and a few on the petals.

SWEET PEA

Cut a petal using a sweet pea cutter. Frill with a cocktail stick, cup each side and attach to the previous petal with egg white. It should look a little like a butterfly.

Cut out another petal with the larger sweet pea cutter. Frill, vein the centre with a modelling tool, and attach with egg white.

Cut a pale green calyx using either a small calyx or star cutter. Attach by threading the wire through the centre and pulling up.

When the flower is completely dry, dust to the desired colour with petal dust or lustre colour.

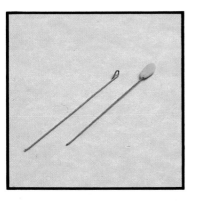

Use pliers to make a small hook in a piece of 26-gauge wire. Dip the hook in egg white, then cover with a very small piece of paste.

Roll out some pale coloured paste and cut the first petal using either a small rose petal cutter or a pansy petal cutter. Attach with egg white down one side, place the first stage into the centre and stick the two halves together. Mould onto the covered hook.

CARNATION

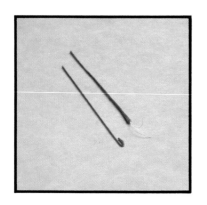

Make a hook in the end of a piece of 26-gauge wire. Cut the tip from a stamen, fold the stamen in half, and attach it to the hook with fine wire. Tape from the end of the hook for about 5cm (2in) down the wire. Run scissors along stamen cotton to curl it.

Roll out some coloured paste. Carnations look best when made in pale pink or cream paste and then petal dusted to a darker shade. Cut with a carnation cutter. Use a sharp modelling knife to make small cuts all around the scalloped edge at regular intervals. Frill with a cocktail stick. Keep turning the paste while working, and apply quite a lot of pressure to get the right effect.

Put some egg white over half of the frilled petal. Thread the prepared wire through the centre of the petal and fold up the other half to make a fan shape. Brush some egg white on the right-hand third and fold over. Turn and repeat on the other side. Mould gently onto the wire.

Cut and frill two more petals. Thread the first one onto the wire, then turn upside-down so that the petal falls in a natural shape onto the head. Repeat with the second petal. Gently mould the base of the petals onto the wire. Leave to dry.

For the calyx, make a cone from green paste. Cut five petals with a knife, then cut to the points with scissors. Thread onto the wire and gently mould round the base of the petals.

Petal dust the dry carnation by working from the outside to the inside to give a greater density of colour on the frilled edges. Alternatively, for a softer look, dust from the inside to the outside. Finish with leaves made from floristry tape or flower paste.

DAISY

Roll out some white paste and cut using a daisy cutter. Use a modelling knife to cut each petal in half.

Frill each half petal using a cocktail stick. Place onto a piece of foam and cup the centre.

Make a hook in the end of a piece of 26-gauge wire. Take a ball of green flower paste, make into a cone and roll out using a paintbrush. Cut with a small calyx cutter. Dip the wire into egg white and pull down through the centre of the calyx. Place a small plug of green paste over the hook.

Place the daisy onto the prepared calyx, sticking with a little egg white. Apply a little pressure to the centre with a modelling tool to ensure that it is firmly stuck.

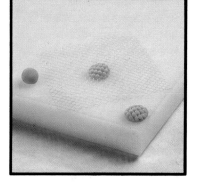

Put a small piece of dark yellow paste on the end of your finger. Pull a piece of tulle over the paste, then attach to the centre of the daisy.

Petal dust the centre and around the base of the petals with moss green colour. Daisies are attractive flowers for spring and summer wedding sprays.

FUCHSIA

Roll out a piece of paste very thinly and cut two petals using a small rose petal cutter. Soften with a cocktail stick and cup slightly.

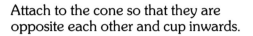

Attach to the cone so that they are opposite each other and cup inwards.

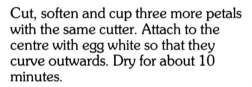

Cut, soften and cup three more petals with the same cutter. Attach to the centre with egg white so that they curve outwards. Dry for about 10 minutes.

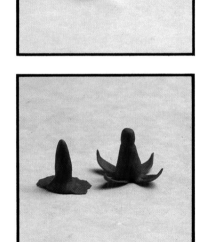

Using a different colour paste, make a cone and turn it into a hat shape. Use a fuchsia cutter to cut the petals. Vein the centre of each petal with a modelling tool. Cup the centre with a ball tool to make the cavity for the first stage. Pull the wire through the centre, attaching the outer petals to the inner ones with egg white.

Petal dust the dried flower and stamens. Dust a little green on the base to represent the calyx. Fuchsias look best when arranged in hanging sprays. They come in many colours and an assortment on a cake looks very attractive.

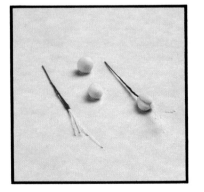

Take four stamens and fold three of them in half. The one longer one is the stigma, and should extend about 5mm (¼in) below the others. Wrap a piece of fine wire around the stamens, then attach to 30-gauge covered wire with floristry tape. Take a pea-sized piece of paste, make into a cone, then place onto the wire by threading the wire through the centre. The thicker end should be at the wire end. Use a cocktail stick or veining tool to mark three lines on the cone.

...UTTER

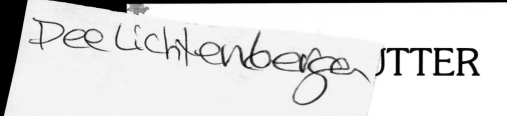

Plunger cutter flowers in three different sizes.

Plunger blossom cutters come in several sizes, and plunger blossom are quicker and easier to make than moulded flowers. First, roll out a small piece of paste very thinly.

Place the plunger cutter on top of the paste and press down. Eject the flower onto a piece of sponge by pressing down on the plunger.

Cut a few stamens in half and thread through the hole in the blossom. If making white flowers, use coloured stamens. Pipe a little royal icing under the stamen head and pull the stamen through so that it is fixed to the flower. Turn upside-down to dry.

Cup the flower using the small end of a ball tool or cranked ball tool. Cut out and cup about 20 flowers in this way. Make a hole in the centre of each blossom with a pin-ended modelling tool or with a large needle. Leave to dry for about 30 minutes.

Wire the blossom into sprays. Usually three large, four medium-sized and five small blossom are included in a spray. Use fine strips of floristry tape to attach each blossom to 10cm (4in) long pieces of 28- or 30-gauge wire, and wire into a spray. Petal dust the finished sprays.

BASIC PULLED FLOWERS

Hand modelled or pulled flowers are made without cutters. The only basic equipment needed is a small wooden pointed stick, such as a cocktail stick or sharpened piece of dowelling, and a sharp modelling knife. The flower shown here is a basic five-petal blossom. The size of the finished flower is determined by the size of the piece of paste. Pulled blossom can also be made with four or six petals.

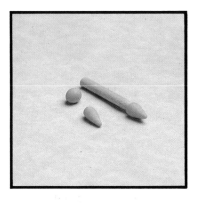

Take a pea-sized piece of paste and make into a cone. Insert the wooden stick into the thick end of the cone.

Use the modelling knife to cut five equal-sized petals from the thick end of the cone.

Take the flower off the stick and open it up by taking each petal in turn and using these three motions:
    Squash: squash the petal between your thumb and forefinger.
    Pinch: pinch the end of the petal to make the edges slightly rounded.
    Pull: Soften and thin the petal by gently pulling the end between your thumb and forefinger, with the thumb on top and forefinger underneath.

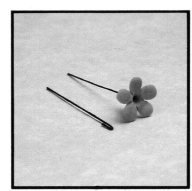

Repeat the squash/pinch/pull motion on all five petals, keeping a uniform size.

Make a hook in the end of a piece of 28- to 30-gauge wire, dip into egg white and pull down through the centre of the flower. Mould the paste onto the wire.

When the blossom is dry, petal dust to the desired shade. These blossoms can be wired into sprays or used as filler flowers in other sprays.

PULLED FREESIAS

Freesias can be made either with cutters or, as shown here, by the hand modelled or pulled flower method. The flowers can either be made in a pale coloured paste, or in cream paste and then petal-dusted to the correct colour when dry.

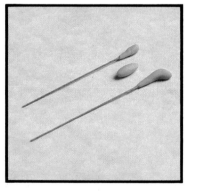

Make some buds first. Take some 26- or 28-gauge wire and make a hook in the end. Dip the hook into egg white and insert into a very small piece of paste. Mould the paste around the hook. Make two or three more buds, each one a little bit larger than the last.

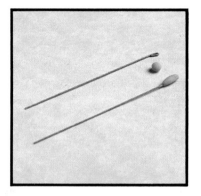

For larger buds, take a slightly enlongated piece of paste and mould onto the wire. Make one or two buds this size. To make a larger one, use a bigger piece of paste and pull the end over slightly.

To make an opening bud, make a large bud as in Step 2, and cut in half with scissors to open. Twist slightly to make it look realistic. Make a few more, depending on how large the spray of freesias will be.

The freesia flowers are made by the same method as the pulled blossom, but with six petals instead of five. Cut the six petals, then squash, pinch and pull each one. Soften the edges by rolling a cocktail stick backwards and forwards on the edges. Place the flower on a piece of sponge and cup the petals with a ball tool.

Pulling from the outside to the inside, insert a hooked wire, bend three of the petals into the centre, and position the other three on top. To make a fully opened flower, make as for Step 4, but place five pieces of stamen cotton in the centre and make the petals more open. Dry all the flowers and buds completely, then colour with petal dust. Paint on the calyxes.

Assemble into a spray, starting by wiring together the smallest buds, then moving onto the flowers, working from left to right. Bend the wire under the last flower to form almost a right angle and hold with a box-shaped piece of floristry tape. Bend to a natural shape.

MORE PULLED FLOWERS

Violet: Cut the cone into five petals, with one petal slightly larger for the tongue. Squash/pinch/pull all the petals, then soften the edges with a cocktail stick. Cup the petals on either side of the tongue using a ball tool. Attach the wire and leave to dry. Dust the finished flower with white and yellow, and add a fine line of yellow royal icing.

Bouvardia: Take a long, thin piece of white or pink paste and mould onto the end of a wooden stick. Cut four equal-sized petals. Squash/pinch/pull the petals to a slight point at the ends. Vein the centre. Mould the flower onto fine wire. For bouvardia buds, mould the paste straight onto the wire. Arrange into a clustered spray.

Cymbidium orchid: Cut the cone into six, with one petal slightly larger than the others. Frill the large petal, and squash/pinch/pull the other five petals. Attach the wire with a right-angled hook, and tuck the frilled lip in at the sides. Add an additional piece of paste to the centre and attach with egg white. Colour the dry flower as desired.

Stephanotis: Take a long piece of paste and mould it onto the end of the wooden stick. Cut five equal petals. Squash/pinch/pull each petal. Vein down the centre. Hook a 26-gauge wire and attach into the centre of the flower. Place a few fine stamens in the centre, and position a green star calyx when the flower is dry. Dust with a little green.

Frilled blossom: Although not a specific flower, these can be made in various sizes and used as filler flowers in sprays. Make a cone of paste, mould onto a wooden stick and cut five equal-sized petals. Squash and pinch, but do not pull the petals. Instead, frill each petal with a cocktail stick. Mould the flower on 28-gauge wire. When dry, petal dust as desired.

Lily of the valley: Take a small piece of white paste and mould onto a small ball tool instead of onto a modelling stick. Cut six small petals. Squash/pinch/pull each petal, then mould the flower onto a 30-gauge wire or onto a stamen. Mould the buds directly onto the wire or stamen. Wire into spray.

VARIEGATED IVY

Ivy is an attractive foliage to include in sugar flower sprays, as it is small and comes in many shades of green. Variegated ivy is ideal, as its delicate shading blends well with most colours. These instructions are for variegated ivy: other ivies and foliage can be made in the same way and then coloured differently.

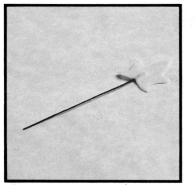

Colour the flower paste ivory or cream. Take a pea-sized ball of paste and squash it between your thumb and forefinger.

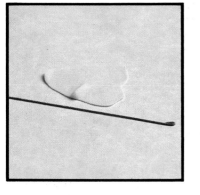

Using a small paintbrush or similar tool, roll the paste from the centre to the outer edge, keeping an area in the centre which is large enough to insert a wire into.

Cut out the leaf with an ivy cutter, placing the base of the cutter over the thickest part of the paste. Take a piece of 28- or 30-gauge wire and make a hook in the end. Dip the hook into a little egg white. Holding the leaf firmly between your thumb and forefinger, carefully insert the wire into the thick part of the paste.

Secure the wire by carefully moulding the paste around it with your fingers or with a cocktail stick.

Vein the leaf using a violet leaf veiner on both sides. Dry on foam or crumpled tissue to create a natural shape. Do not dry flat, as the leaf will be stiff and un-natural.

Paint the dry leaf. The idea is to build up the variegation by using three or four tones of green. Dilute some moss green colouring with clear alcohol to make a weak coloured solution. Paint the leaf all over on both sides, working from the centre to the outside edge. Leave some cream on the edges. When dry, add a bit more colour and add some darker shading. Continue until a realistic variegation is created.

CHRISTMAS CAKE

This royal-iced Christmas cake
features an unusual spray of
winter jasmine, ivy, holly and
mistletoe.

FOLIAGE AND FILLER FLOWERS

Many different leaf shapes can be made from floristry tape. Leaves made from tape are particularly useful and very effective when used to represent the foliage of such flowers as mimosa, fuchsia, jasmine and carnations when these flowers are wired into sprays. The foliage of these flowers when made from flower paste may shatter when wired into complicated sprays, but making foliage from floristry tape allows the sprays to be wired tightly without breakages.

To make floristry tape foliage, use sharp scissors to cut out a realistic shape and size for the leaf. Pull a cocktail stick or leaf veiner down the centre to add strength to the leaf. The leaves can either be used wired or unwired in the sprays. If necessary, the tape can be made wider by sticking two pieces together with confectioner's glaze or gum arabic glue.

Mimosa: Mimosa looks attractive when used as a filler in sugar flower sprays, particularly sprays of spring flowers. Colour the flower paste yellow and make into pea-sized balls. For each ball, make a hook in the end of a piece of covered 30-gauge wire. Thread through the paste and secure it onto the wire. Dip the paste into egg white, and then dip into yellow petal dust or coloured caster sugar. Arrange into a realistic shape and tape together several flowers. Make the foliage from floristry tape.

Gypsophila: Gypsophila is a popular inclusion for wedding sprays, as it helps to soften the effect of brightly coloured flowers. Make hooks in the ends of 30-gauge covered wire, dip into egg white, and mould tiny pieces of white paste over each hook. For each flower, squash a small sausage of paste between your thumb and forefinger. Roll with a paintbrush, then frill with a cocktail stick. Put some egg white down the frilled edge, place the paste-covered wire at one end, and roll up to make the flowers, which should look a little like miniature carnations. Wire several flowers and buds into a spray and use a fine paintbrush dipped in green food colour to paint on the calyxes.

An assortment of sugar foliage made by the same technique for making variegated ivy.

TRADITIONAL BRIDAL BOUQUET

The flowers and foliage used in this spray are wired roses, carnations, stephanotis, freesias, gypsophila and variegated ivy.

Start wiring at the bottom by taping together several ivy leaves. Tape in some stephanotis, freesias and their buds, add some ribbons, then tape in a rose and a carnation.

Continue wiring the spray, bending to an attractive curved shape. Add filler flowers and foliage where needed to fill out the shape.

Build up the spray with more roses and carnations, surrounded by stephanotis and freesias. Fill out the shape with gypsophila, and wire in ivy and ribbon loops.

Finish the bouquet with ribbon loops, long trailing ribbons, and butterflies on wires fluttering over the cake. It may be easier to add the butterflies once the spray is in position on the cake.

REVERSED S-CURVE

This reversed S-curve has been made using miniature flowers. You will need five miniature orchids, 18 assorted-sized pulled blossom, six frilled blossom, nine buds, seven small ivy leaves and some ribbon loops.

The flowers used to make up this spray are pulled blossom, frilled blossom, ivy and miniature orchid.

Wire together a small posy, leaving two cavities for the legs of the spray.

Start by making the upper leg of the spray. Take a single bud, then tape in another two buds.

Tape in the ribbon loops to fill out the spray and give a rounded, even shape.

Start adding pulled blossom, frilled blossom, an ivy leaf and finish with a miniature orchid. Make an identical leg for the bottom, but work so that the spray is a mirror image of the first one.

Tape in the legs, and use some blossom as filler flowers.

V-SHAPED SPRAY

The V-shaped spray looks attractive on a round or hexagonal cake. This one is made using carnations, blossom, pulled flowers and ivy. Start by making two identical legs. Wire in buds, smaller flowers, foliage and finish with a carnation. The second leg should be a mirror image of the first, and an easy way to do this is to wire everything the same, then move the flowers to the other side of the spray. Wire the legs together. Make a posy with three carnations, tiny flowers and ribbon loops, and wire it in the centre.

CORSAGE

A corsage looks delicate on a small cake, or it can be used as a sugarcraft gift on a place card or instead of a bow on a wrapped package. The corsage shown here has a focal point of a single pink orchid, but another fairly large flower could also be used. Wire together with foliage such as ivy, some gypsophila, some ribbon loops and some bows with tails.

STRAIGHT SPRAY

This is probably the most common spray, and one of the easiest to make. Simply wire the flowers so that they increase in size, starting with buds and blossom and finishing with larger flowers and foliage, the largest at the bottom, adding 3mm (⅛in) ribbon bows. The pretty spray here includes roses, gypsophila, ivy and pulled blossom and stephanotis.

VASE OF FLOWERS

Choose a small vase and fill it with sugarpaste. Fill with several ribbon loops and trailers to get an even, rounded shape, then add plunger flowers and pulled blossom. Use on top of a cake or as a free-standing table decoration.

POSY

AUSTRALIAN-STYLE RIBBON LOOP

Posies are round sprays which look best placed in the centre of a fairly large round cake. A Victorian posy has a rose as the focal point. Round flowers such as roses or carnations work best in a posy, and there are usually either three or five main flowers included. Start by taping together three blossom. Add two ribbon loops.

Keeping working in this way, going round in a circle adding larger flowers, buds and blossom, and taking care to keep the shape. When the desired size is reached, add some trailing ribbons and place in a frill or posy holder. Tape around the wires to cover them and attach to the holder.

This spray is assembled directly into a small piece of sugarpaste stuck onto the surface of the cake using clear alcohol. The spray shown has been made using silk flowers, but it can also be made with sugar flowers. Follow an exact pattern, beginning with the ribbons. There should be a cross in the centre, then an eight-point star. Finish with two ribbon loops with tails. When the ribbons are arranged, place the flowers in position, sticking the wires firmly into the sugarpaste.

TULLE

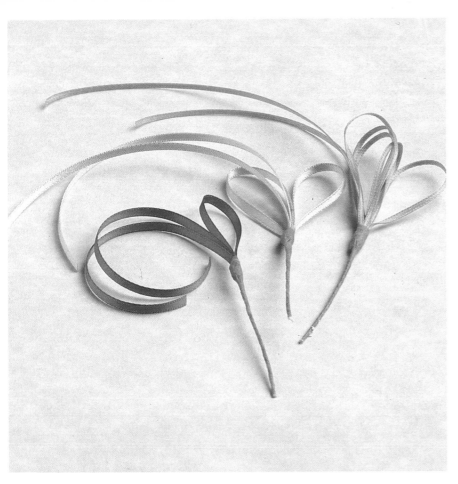

Like ribbon, tulle has many uses in cake decorating. It can be used for tulle piping objects such as booties and flowers, as a frill to go around a cake, for bows, or as a filler in sugar flower sprays. Buy bridal tulle, which is very soft and dainty. Nylon net is too stiff, especially for use in sprays.

To make tulle bows, cut a small rectangle of tulle. Gather up the centre with your fingers. Place a piece of 28-gauge wire over the tight gathers, bend it over and twist tightly. Tulle bows look particularly attractive with flowers such as orchids, as they can soften sprays and corsages.

AMERICAN-STYLE WEDDING CAKE

In this American-style cake the top tier is placed on the bottom tier rather than being supported on pillars or a stand.

SUGAR FLOWER BOXES

Small rectangular box topped with pink fabric flowers.

A square box tied with ribbon and decorated with apple blossom, pulled blossom, fabric leaves and dried sea lavender.

Tie a box with gold cord and insert a spray of pulled blossom.

Square box featuring looped ribbon bows topped with blossom.

FAVOURS

To make the tulle bags, cut circles of tulle using a saucer or plate for a pattern. Fill with sugared almonds, as shown, or small sweets or chocolates, gather together and tie or wire, leaving a long frill at the top. Decorate with sugar fuchsias, plunger cutter blossom or cutter flowers and tie with matching ribbons.

A tiny posy of dried miniature rosebuds and sugar foliage.

Another square box tied with matching ribbon and decorated with a small arrangement of pulled blossom, variegated ivy and freesias.

SWEETS

Pipe tiny flowers onto sugarcubes, sugared almonds or after-dinner mints as a special touch for a wedding or dinner party.

KNIFE

For a special birthday cake or wedding, decorate the knife with a spray of sugar flowers to match the spray on the cake. Attach to the knife with florist's wire, then cover the wire with ribbons to match the spray.

TABLE SETTING

As well as decorating cakes and other food, sugar flowers can be used to make delicate and unusual table decorations. The sugar flowers can be made to co-ordinate with the colour schemes for a dinner party table, to match a fresh flower centrepiece, or to match the spray on a celebration cake.

Decorate a napkin ring with a small spray of briar roses, blossom and foliage. Attach to the ring with softened flower paste, then allow to harden before use. Store wrapped in tissue paper in a box kept in a cool place.

Make the place card holder from a sugarpaste rectangle and leave it to harden completely. Use a crimper to make a line for the paper to be inserted. Decorate with a tiny spray of flowers to match the

rest of the decorations. Make a small sugarpaste triangle for the base support. These can be stored wrapped in tissue paper.

Decorate a simple china candlestick holder with a ring of wired miniature briar roses. Arrange them together with blossom made using a plunger cutter. Stick the wires into sugarpaste or florist's clay so that the sugar flowers can be removed from the candlestick.

INSTRUCTIONS
FOR CAKES

Wedding cake with fresh flowers: A different way of decorating the two-tiered heart shaped wedding cake, this time using the fresh flower bridal bouquet. Decorate the top tier with embroidery instead of lace, and position a posy pick so that the bride's bouquet can be placed on the cake after the ceremony.

Piped flower cake: Pipe a large assortment of royal icing flowers in various sizes and shapes. Leave to dry thoroughly. Mark a circle on top of the cake. It should be about 5cm (2in) smaller than the diameter of the cake, and the easiest way to mark it is to place a suitably-sized thin cake board on the surface and mark around it with a scriber or a hat pin.
Fill a medium-sized piping bag with green royal icing and attach a leaf tube, or cut to a W-shape.

Pipe leaves around the marked circle, covering 5-7.5cm (2-3in) at a time and attaching the flowers as you go. Try to get a good flow of colour around the ring. When finished, use a No1 piping tube with pink icing to pipe embroidery around the flowers. Pipe around the base with a No2 tube and either green or white icing. Attach 1cm (⅜in) ribbon around the side, tie the bow and curl the ends.

Heart wedding cake:
The cake is covered in ivory sugarpaste and decorated with scallops of lace in the shape of miniature bows. Piped doves and flooded embroidery are featured on the surface of the bottom tier, while butterflies on fine wire flutter above the sugar bouquet on the top tier.

Fortieth anniversary or birthday cake: Coat the cake with white sugarpaste. For the side decoration, cut a piece of soft bridal tulle about twice the circumference of the cake. Roll it up loosely, then cut a scallop on one edge. When unfolded, the scalloped pattern will be repeated the length of the tulle. Take a needle and cotton, and gather up the straight edge using a running stitch. Tie the ends of cotton to position the tulle around the cake, then attach with royal icing, holding the gathers as you go.

Plait together two colours of ribbon and a piece of silver twine, and attach above the tulle with royal icing. Finish off with some miniature bows and tiny rose buds. Push the posy pick in the surface of the cake and arrange the ribbons, The number 40 is a run-out. Paint silver when dry. Pipe the filigree butterfly.

Pink birthday cake: Cover the cake with pale pink sugarpaste. Make the pinks following the instructions for carnations, but cut with a medium-sized primula cutter. Before attaching the petals, paint or dust the inside with dark pink colouring, as it will be impossible to do so when the flower is assembled. To make buds, place a piece of pink paste in a cone of green paste, attach onto wire and mould to shape. Cut the top with a modelling knife to give the effect of an opening bud.

Attach the flowers to the cake. Roll out some long, thin pieces of green paste for stems and attach to the cake surface with a little egg white or clear alcohol. Make foliage from curled strips of paste. Make a glue from green flower paste mixed with egg white, and attach the pinks to the cake. Add a sugarpaste label. Finish off with embroidery, a small snailstrail and ribbon round the base.

Peach engagement cake: The doves and inscription are piped on the top. Finish off the sides with ribbon insertion, embroidered bows and tiny flowers.

American-style wedding cake: Cover both tiers with pale lemon sugarpaste. Place the top tier on a piece of card the same size as the base and attach to the bottom tier with a small piece of sugarpaste.

Pipe a snailstrail around the base of the cake and where the two tiers join. Attach the frills and decorate with miniature green bows.

The large wired spray is made with daisies, ivy and pulled blossom. Stick into a posy pick inserted in the top of the cake. Once the spray is in position, put some pale lemon sugarpaste over the base and smooth over with a palette knife to cover both the pick and the hole. Finish off the cake with piped doves and green velvet ribbon.

Christmas cake: For the side design, pipe holly using green icing and a No1 tube, then pipe red dots for berries with a No0 or 1. Pipe a shell around the base. The top edge has small running scrolls piped with a No42, then overpiped with a No2. Wire the spray, adding red and green ribbon loops. Pipe an inscription if liked.